Stop the Ship!

To Hong Kong!

Written by Joanna Layland

My top fact!

This is Hong Kong.
It is buzzing!

2

It has lots of ships.
This ship is a junk ship.

Lots of bots fit in this box! I can sell them.

The bots munch a lot.
It is a BIG problem!

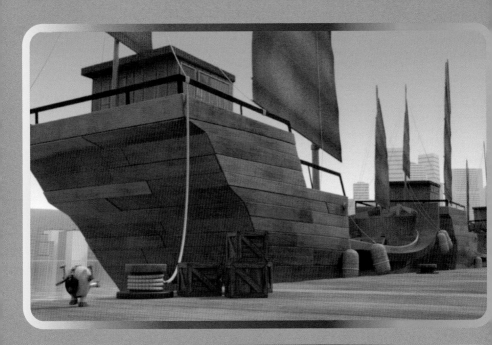

munch!

They munch and let
the junk ships go.

The big ship
must not hit
the junk ships!

Quick! Stop
the crash!

Bots! Help me get the junk ships!

Grab this, Foz!

They get the junk
ships to the dock.